external affairs

By the same author

*(*Published by New Island/South Dublin County Council as part of INCONTEXT3)*

Comhairle Contae
Átha Cliath Theas
South Dublin County Council

The *Night & Day* sequence by Dermot Bolger was commissioned
under South Dublin County Council's INCONTEXT3 Programme
which is funded by the Department of Environment Heritage and
Local Government and the National Roads Authority.

Comhshaol, Oidhreacht agus Rialtas Áitiúil
Environment, Heritage and Local Government

National Roads Authority
An tÚdarás um Bóithre Náisiúnta

Contents

III The Frost is All Over

IV Three Poems

Born in Dublin in 1959, Dermot Bolger's nine novels include **The Woman's Daughter, The Journey Home, Father's Music, The Valparaiso Voyage** and most recently **The Family on Paradise Pier.** His debut play, **The Lament for Arthur Cleary**, received The Samuel Beckett Award and the first of his Ballymun Trilogy, **From These Green Heights**, won the Irish Times/ESB Award for Best New Irish Play of 2004. Author of eight volumes of poetry, he has been Playwright in Association with the Abbey Theatre and Writer Fellow in Trinity College, Dublin. He devised the best-selling collaborative novels, **Finbar's Hotel** and **Ladies Night at Finbar's Hotel** and has edited many anthologies including **The Picador Book of Contemporary Irish Fiction.**

As a resident artist in South Dublin County Council's INCONTEXT3 Percent for Art Programme, he wrote **Walking the Road**, a play which explores the life of the poet Francis Ledwidge and, through him, the forgotten lives of young men from South Dublin County who died in the First World War. Published by New Island Books in association with INCONTEXT3, **Walking the Road** has been staged to acclaim in Ireland, Belgium, The USA and Britain.

His **Night & Day** sequence which is published here has also been merged with work by over two dozen fellow writers to present a portrait of Dublin life over twenty-hour hours in the illustrated anthology **Night & Day** (New Island/South Dublin County Council) which is being published to coincide with this book.

Author's Note

The poem sequence *Night & Day* which forms the centrepiece of this collection, was first published as large posters or as wall murals in locations as diverse as Luas tram stops in Tallaght or the gable of the Cunas and Cairdeas Centre in Neilstown in North Clondalkin – which houses the local Drugs Task Force and where the poem *Neilstown Matadors* is set. It was a rare privilege to sometimes position poems in the locations that inspired them. Poetry will rarely affect a broad constituency when displayed in any public space. But I was seeking the one person in five hundred who turns a familiar corner and is surprised to see some hint of their own experience reflected back from a wall. These posters and murals became my way of leaving the sort of sign that I had longed for as a youth, an affirmation of the validity of seeing things in a different way.

Night & Day forms a succession of snapshots taken on the run amid the flow of busy lives. They were commissioned under South Dublin County Council's INCONEXT3 percent for art public art scheme. This scheme allowed me time to be an observer, to journey through Clondalkin and Rathfarnham and Tallaght and imaginatively reinvent the thoughts of a woman glimpsed waiting for a tram or a foreign worker alighting from one, a teenage girl on a street, a man walking alone at night, a women trapped in the glacier of a motorway bottle-neck, the people we generally pass and forget, people whose lives I had the imaginative space to speculate about or people I met who told me about their lives.

The aim of INCONTEXT3 was to commission public art of excellence in South Dublin County, to allow artists the time and opportunity to explore new ways of working and allow communities to find new ways of connecting with this work. Poems, by their nature, rarely form part of any visual land-scape. They are private acts, generally about private emotions. My challenge was to create a sequence of poems that was public and private, both internal and external.

I attempted this in several ways. By initially being published in unexpected places, the poems formed the pages of a public book left open on gable ends or at station platforms. This allowed the poems to sometimes take on inde-pendent lives, like when schoolchildren used one to decorate their school library or a class of mature adults returning to education created their own mural based on *Graffiti on a Corner*.

Also wherever these poems first appeared – be it in local parish newsletters, as posters in libraries, theatre foyers or motor tax offices, or as words and video images projected onto pavements in Tallaght and Clondalkin at night – they contained an invitation for writers who lived or worked in South Dublin County to join in this imaginative journey by sending me original poems so that they would become my co-authors in a separate anthology, which posi-tions my poems in the context of fellow writers working around me.

Therefore my *Night & Day* sequence is being published twice, because these poems also appear in an anthology entitled *Night & Day* (New Island/South Dublin County Council, 2008) in which they deliberate form only one half of a story as they are interwoven into a far broader tapestry of other voices that hopefully capture some of contemporary life in South Dublin County today. Many of the submitted poems for that *Night & Day* anthology brim with a sense of their authors' lives and on this level they are probably "truer" in an autobiographical sense than mine. Because most of my poems are external in the sense of generally being observational and speculative, fictional in that they are written in the voices of others. I tried to strip away the "I" from my poetry and use instead the "eye" through which we perpetually observe fellow commuters or strangers on the street, people with whom we share busy lifts or supermarket check-out queues, people whose lives we find ourselves unconsciously speculating about.

Having placed them in that broader context in the *Night & Day* anthology, here in *External Affairs* they are published in the context of the other poems that I have been writing and the other lives I have tried to capture in recent years.

The opening section of *External Affairs* contains *Ballymun Incantation,* a poem composed to be recited by actors and local people as the centrepiece of a public wake on the eve of the demolition of the first tower block in the Dublin suburb of Ballymun in the summer of 2004. In a performance directed by Ray Yeates of **axis** Art and Community Resource Centre, it was recited by Máire Ní Ghrainne, Kelly Hickey and the late Derek Fitzpatrick. *Travel Light* was read by the actor Vincent McCabe at the opening of the Dublin Port Tunnel, in a performance also directed by Ray Yeates.

The Frost is All Over sequence also deals with external lives. Almost all the tunes that form the bedrock of Irish traditional music were collected in book form in 1903 and 1907 by Francis O'Neill – the Chicago chief of police who made it his life's work to rescue a music that seemed about to be lost. Tunes once played in Donegal kitchens or at wakes in the Knockmealdown Mountains where written down in tenements in Chicago or in taverns where customers ignored O'Neill's rank and O'Neill ignored their crimes, both accepting that they were linked by a shared respect for music.

In 2006 the acclaimed musician Tony McMahon approached me to write a sequence of poems to be interlinked with his own accordion playing and the playing of the uilleann piper David Power. *The Frost is All Over* sequence tries to explore the ever deepening relationship between musicians and the tunes that they play throughout their lives. It is also a remembrance of the custodians of that music. Players like Patsy Toughey, who survived by playing his pipes amid the slapstick of American Vaudeville or Seamus Ennis who criss-crossed Ireland and Britain with a set of pipes originally found by his father in a sack in a London pawnbrokers. It is a celebration too of less known singers like Mary Ann Carolan who kept the music alive in Louth, or Sonny Brogan who kept an open house for musicians in his small terraced Dublin home.

The suite of poems became part of a multi-media performance, entitled *The Frost is All Over* which centres on the playing of Tony McMahon and David Power. It was first produced in 2008 by David Teevan of Ten.24 Productions and directed by John Comiskey.

I would like to express my gratitude to the support team behind INCONTEXT3, to Rachel McAree, Claire Nidecker, Sarah Searson, Colette Ryan, to Caroline Orr who was there at the start, and to Orla Scannell, South Dublin County Council's Arts Officer, who has been a hugely supportive presence. I would like to thank Leo Duffy, James Keane and all the design team at Yellowstone Communications and Edwin Higel and everyone at New Island Books. My thanks to Fiona Ness, Helen Boylan and Nadine O'Regan, who published the *Night & Day* poems as a monthly sequence (under the title *County Lives*) in the *Sunday Business Post*. My thanks to the constantly supportive staff of South Dublin County's Public Library Service in whose branches many of these poems were displayed. Similarly to the staff of the Civic Theatre in Tallaght, the Quarryvale Community and Leisure Centre, the Quarryvale Family Resource Centre, Rowlagh Parish Church, Clondalkin Civic Offices and Motor Tax

Office, Tymon Park Visitors Centre, Property Path, the Tallaght Institute of Technology, Collinstown Park Community College, Collinstown Park Sport and Community Centre, Ronanstown Youth Service, Ronanstown CPD, the Get Ahead (After School) Club, Neilstown, the Cumas and Cairdeas Centre, Neilstown and Honeybears Crèche in Quarryvale (who found space for two specially written children's poems not included here). My thanks also to Laura Flynn, Landscape Architect with the Railway Procurement Agency; to the artist Peter Farrell who created a wonderful video projection based on the poem "*Woman Waiting for the Luas*", screened onto the pavement in Clondalkin and Tallaght, to *The North Clondalkin Buzz* (The North Clondalkin Community Development Project newsletter), *The Irish Times* and *The Sunday Independent* who published individual poems after they had first appeared on posters and murals and to the Clondalkin Gazette who distributed *Neilstown Matadors* as a free poster insert.

A special and sincere thanks to Fiona Delaney, South Dublin County Council Arts Development Worker in North Clondalkin who curated many of the poems here as a separate strand entitled *The Clondalkin Suite*, and who worked so closely with the North Clondalkin community in selecting the indoor and outdoor locations where they were displayed. Sincere thanks also to John Carpenter, the talented mural artist, who created the wall murals that incorporated many of these poems within them.

Dermot Bolger,
October 2008

I

Ballymun Incantation & Travel Light

Ballymun Incantation

Whose voice can you hear?
Who calling down the stair?
What ghost trapped in a lift shaft?
What child who played and laughed?

In nineteen hundred and sixty seven,
Craning our necks towards heaven,
We arrived here by truck and bus,
Three thousand families of us.

Tea chests and cardboard suitcases,
Boxes bound with old shoelaces,
From tenements in condemned streets,
Now the world appeared at our feet.

Crowding the lifts and up each stair,
Onto the balconies to breathe the air,
We were so dizzy all Dublin spun:
The chosen families of Ballymun.

I think this heat is killing us.
Why can't we turn off the radiators?
Where are the shops we were promised?
Why won't they come to fix the broken lifts?

My name is Mary, when I turned nine
I slept alone for the first time,
My sister whispering secrets overhead
In Ceannt Tower in a new bunk bed.

In Plunkett Tower my wife grew shook,
She was alone when the lift got stuck,
She hated the squatters jarring her nerves,
I still see her shaking, reciting prayers.

My name is Agnes, when I was born
The Civil War was still raging on.
I moved to Balcurris with my grandchildren,
I lived for Novenas and Sweet Afton.

My name is John, I stole my first kiss
Just before the doors opened in the lift
Eilish was still in her school uniform
Surely no other love could be this strong.

Help me, I'm still lost here and all alone,
I injected my mother's hopes into my arm,
Shivering in the depths of cold turkey
I thought I could fly from this balcony.

Why won't the voices stop whispering,
Straining to be heard amid the babbling?
Lives that were ended and lives begun,
The living and the dead of Ballymun.

Remember my name, it is Elizabeth,
In the local workhouse I faced my death.
Cholera stole away my famished son,
I buried him amid the fields of Ballymun.

Remember me, my ghost also haunts here,
Seeking my child who fell through the air.
The coroner declared my death was suicide,
I just wanted to be my dead daughter's side.

I loved the marches during the rent strikes,
All us boys riding behind on chopper bikes,
It was brilliant there laughing with my mates,
That's where I asked Joan for our first date.

Every touch and every thrust and every kiss
Every feud, every fight, every lip split,
Every face lost at the window of a tower block
Every loan shark with a list of women in hock.

Every whiskey, every Valium, every cigarette,
Every couple holding hands in a kitchenette,
Every laughing child being spun in the August sun
Every boy with a piebald horse to gallop on.

Every mother dreaming about some different life,
Every first tooth, first communion, every surgeon's knife,
Every welder, office cleaner, every unemployed,
Every girl who fought back when her dreams died.

Every young poet who wrote it out in verse:
McDonagh and MacDermott, Connolly and Pearse,
Every name scrawled on walls in each tower block,
Every face that is remembered, every face forgot,

Every life that ended here and every life begun:
The living and the dead of Ballymun.

Travel Light

It hung on a nail in the shed, my father's travel light bag,
When not being carried to the gates of Alexandra Dock

By bus from Liberty Hall, containing his clothes and alarm clock:
All the necessities in the condensed life of a ship's cook

Who paused on the gangplank to watch crane drivers load
Containers bound for Hamburg, Le Havre and Rotterdam.

How many pairs of hands led to those goods being stowed,
With my father's crew one link in an army of transportation?

How many men were needed before the Port Tunnel was complete,
How many daughters helped mothers pack a holdall or travel-light,

How many sons carried suitcases to the corner of a street,
And waved until their fathers had long passed beyond sight?

How many workers reached this land, from which many once left,
To ensure the everyday miracle of the consignments that arrive

When the world is asleep or too engrossed in its own concerns
To be aware of factory hands packing them, of hauliers who drive

Down carriageways ruled by white lines and lined by embankments;
Of stevedores and crane drivers, fork lift operators and ship-hands;

Of tunnellers striving against mudstone, striving for entitlements,
Emerging at the Coolock interchange to yearn for distant homelands.

Five thousand workers built this tunnel, how many thousand will count
Down the long beads of florescent light in cab windows as they traverse

Fairview Park and East Wall, passing under Marino and Beaumont
Inside this invisible chute while life passes by overhead, oblivious.

But behind every shipment is the tunneller who moved the earth,
Who excavated glacier deposits of boulder clay on conveyor belts;

There is a father, like my father, forced to miss his son's birth
As he aligned the precast segments by screwing in spear bolts,

There is a planner, an engineer, a crew servicing the cutting head
That rotated every seventeen seconds through limestone rock;

There is a haulier hypnotised by cat's eyes stretching ahead;
A sailor on deck watching the lights of Dublin port contract;

There is a family in a foreign land awaiting a money transfer;
There are phone calls from Internet cafes and hostel steps;

There is a son at a corner watching his father's departure;
A patchwork of absences criss-crossing the globe at night;

An empty hook in countless homes hammered into a shed door,
Waiting to hold a rucksack, a suitcase or a battered travel-light.

II

Night & Day

On the 7am Luas to Tallaght

I never thought that the West would be like this:
Trying to sleep on the tram to Tallaght at dawn,
My mouth so dry I can no longer taste your kiss.

Swapping words in ten languages for tiredness,
Fellow passengers stare out, barely able to yawn:
They never thought the West would be like this.

This journey compounds every ache of loneliness.
I close my eyes, unable to stop thinking of home,
My mouth so dry I can no longer taste your kiss.

Last night on the phone I could sense your stress,
Our children no longer asking when will I come:
I never thought that the West would be like this.

To them I'm now a cheque from a foreign address,
A man who builds apartments we could never own,
My mouth so dry I can no longer taste your kiss.

All day I will shovel cement, yearning to caress
Your neck with each button of your blouse undone:
I never thought that the West would be like this,
My mouth so dry I can no longer taste your kiss.

Woman Waiting for the Luas, Tallaght, 8.20am

Collect my black skirt from the dry cleaners,
Then party napkins, potty trainers, crackers
For cheese and wine when parents collect
All the new friends Sarah made at the crèche:
Toilet rolls, paper towel to mop up party spills,
Foil-wrapped choc lollipops for going home bags,
Hoover bags, choc drops so our dog with bad breath
Won't start sighing, also feeling left out and slighted:
Sunday's dinner, a DVD I might persuade John to watch
When we're finally alone – his birthday princess put to bed:
Something, anything, to remind him then that I still exist.

Traffic Flow

Traffic-flow, traffic stutter, traffic halt:
Stalled faces lit by green light from the dash.

Have I sat here before and experienced this dawn
In some dream or other life, or does my imagination

Confuse it with every other morning of every week?
Taillights flicker across a landscape of no escape,

Of embankments blocking off new apartment blocks:
I spend more time here than I spend talking to my wife,

I know the faces here better than I know my neighbours:
The stoic Buddhists of the inner lane and the swines

Using the bus lane to cheat their way in, music blaring.
Those of us not yet beyond caring hope they get scurvy,

Haemorrhoids, penile dysfunction, thrush and beriberi:
Hope that the DJ on Spin FM chokes on his Cornflakes,

Hope the traffic may eventually move, hope we finally reach
Whatever place we scurry to in this slow-motion rush.

We fantasise about one dawn arising from our car to scale
This daffodil-encrusted bank, ignoring startled horns,

As we shout, amid a skyline of cranes:
Look on me, Lord, not just some motorist

But a soul with free will, on my knees in white shirt sleeves,
Raging against this sense of entrapment with my fists.

The Most Washed SUV on the Templeogue Road

This is paradise, the only time that I truly own:
This solitary hour when I let my mind drift,

Stuck in this traffic, safe from her "must do" list
Pinned up in the kitchen with a fridge magnet.

Nobody notices me here as I hum favourite hits,
Fantasise about female motorists and recollect

The elation of struggling with straps, when girls
Let me undress them, frill by silky frill, on nights

When I was more constant than any Northern star,
When evenings brimmed with the possibilities

Of what fate might hold, what doors might open in bedsits,
Where kisses tasted of lipstick and Benson and Hedges.

Could I have envisaged then being captive in a car at dawn,
Content inside my prison, happy to be bullied and bossed,

Knowing that without my jailer I would be truly lost?
She controls time and motion until I strap on my seat belt

At eight a.m. – or earlier if I can invent reports of gridlock.
When I arrive home at six she'll badger me out to the shed

That needs sorting, the lawn needing trimming, on her list
Where life can be ticked off into an ordered happiness.

Sometimes when she bends at the sink I want to lift her dress
Like that afternoon in her father's shed in her tennis skirt,

Only now she would tut and give me her "act your age" eyes.
I don't want to be my age, I want to sit here and fantasise

About convent girls or curing cancer or scoring tries
With a packed crowd hysterical in the corner where I lie

Bruised and sore, but ready to hold the ball aloft
Amid jubilant team mates, with the Triple Crown won,

Cures found for blindness, malaria, middle-age disgruntlement,
The mystery unsolved of the burglar who stole her fridge magnet,

Struggles with bra clasps at seventeen, fishnet stocking worn
By a Leitrim girl in a Rathgar flat, the illicit taste of woodbines,

A hand under the table in Zavargo's Nite Club, mysterious rust
Affecting the tools in our shed, with even the lawn-mower bust,

Our garden gone to pot, a power-cut and her whisper: *"I'm scared,*
Let's go to bed by candlelight. With no other heat in our residence

We must burn my to-do list to stay warm, unless you've other ways
To keep me warm, like on that afternoon I wore a tennis skirt,

And was correcting your pronunciation of 'Duice' when you grasped
Me tight about the waist in the shed amid Daddy's potting plants."

Her sweetness to which I surrounded everything, except my daily fix
Of sitting here staring at taillights, with no boss to supervise

This off-duty hour when I truly exist – midway between my desk
And henpecked life – the hero of the story, free to do as he likes.

The Swimmer at Thirty-Five

(For Caroline Orr)

The moment I hit the water I am in my element:
I was born for this, for backstroke and butterfly.
Born to hold my breath for the entire first length,

During which I slide out from my everyday skin
To again become a Leinster Schoolgirl champion,
All Ireland gold medallist and Olympic contender.

On childhood mornings in my father's old banger
There was no traffic like this, nobody else awake,
Just the pair of us wrapped up in a code of splits

In the pool that opened early merely to let me train.
Chlorine and silence, the sense of being special,
The clarity of light when I stepped into the dawn

With the world only half-wake, as groggy-eyed
As the commuters now look in this tailback of traffic.
But while everyone looked stale, I never felt more alive

Then donning my school uniform to sit at a desk,
Reciting lap-times, my skin glowing with such health
That I could not envisage being daunted by any task.

I'd no time for boyfriends and barely time for friends.
Classmates marvelled at how I coped with having no life,
But that was my life, I could imagine no existence then

Outside of that cocoon controlled by a stopwatch,
Where all problems were solved by simply going faster.
The lane kept clear, nothing allowed to block my path,

No tantrums, no silences, no waiting lists for doctors,
No grammar of autism to slowly learn to comprehend,
No son terrified of swimming, even with armbands,

Cocooned in his world that contains no stop-watches,
No sense of time, no admittance granted to strangers.
I drive my child to day-care centres and specialists

On choked roads like this and while I curse the traffic
He stares out blankly as if half watching a dull film.
I love him and he loves me, even if he cannot show it.

In some dreams I see him dive into a pool and glide
In my slipstream, made graceful by a floating world.
But he screams if he even sees me pack my swim gear.

In my local pool strangers stare twice a week, transfixed
By my apparent speed. But to me it feels like slow motion
As I blunder into beginners who clutter up my lane.

Why do I waste my precious hours of parole there?
Perhaps because occasionally amid a tumble-turn
I block out this constant sense of impeded helplessness,

And become the perfect swimmer, effortlessly omnipotent,
Moving with ease, barely needing to draw breath:
No disappointment can touch me in my element.

Lucan Weir

Will you walk with me here, beside Lucan weir,
Past flowering rush, kingfishers, green figwort,

Your palm so young in mine, your palm frayed with age:
Each generation a whirling leaf sluiced into this cascade.

Will you recall the ordinary afternoon when we paused,
Amid the rush of busy lives, to stare at the torrential spume,

Hypnotised by the ceaseless deluge, until in fact it seemed
That what remained constant and static was this surging weir,

With all our joys, our dreams, our lives spiralling past,
Down each speeded-up season, each irreclaimable year.

In a Clondalkin Supermarket Car Park

Screw all self-appointed martyrs,
Ignore their beguiling monuments:
Screw any ghosts with the neck
To impose upon their descendants
The mortgage of any emotive debt,
Any cloying duty of remembrance
That turns the past into an excuse
To hold us to ransom in the present.

Let the weight of history seem as light
As a party balloon slipping from the grasp
Of a child distracted in a crowded car park.
Let it float above cars choking exit lanes
Until tribal braves become blue specks,
So indistinct amid a skyline of cranes
That they cannot be hijacked from the grave
As tools to be used to justify or condemn.

The child watches her balloon disappear,
She does not stamp her feet or simper;
She lets the past go, being too enthralled
By all the possible futures that await her.

Neilstown Matadors

Super models would kill to be this thin.
The diet is stress, cigarettes and coffee.
My child-raising days should be done,
But somebody had to step into the breach,
Somebody had to pick up the scarlet cloak
And hold it in front of the rampaging bull.

Old spectators in the bull rings of Mexico
Pay no heed to fearless young toreadors
Who imagine themselves to be invincible.
Their interest only stirs after a fighter is gored,
Because only when he re-enters the arena
Will they witness his true test of character.

Some afternoons after school in this room,
Waiting to see the Drugs Taskforce worker,
When my granddaughter suddenly smiles,
When she looks up from her colouring book
With eyes that match my daughter's eyes,
With eyes knowing nothing yet of the danger
Of dealers peddling needs that need to be fed,
With quizzical eyes that I would kill to protect,
She asks the question that she loves to ask:
"Gran, what did you do before you did this?"

What did I do before I took on her welfare?

I fought to raise a daughter on these streets,
I stood in queues and worked on checkouts,
I searched for my child on dangerous estates,
I stood up to debt collectors calling to my door,
When she shivered in detox I tried to nurse her,
I sold my possessions or saw them all robbed,
I cried until one night there were no tears left,

I prayed with what remained of my ebbing faith,
In time I wrapped my grandchild into my arms
And took the place of the person I loved most,
I made a nest amid the belongings I possess,
I stood up in the ring every time I was gored,
I watched the bulls run and raised my cloak
Repeatedly to provide what shelter I could,
I picked myself up and wiped off the blood,
I waited at the school gate to take her hand
So that, walking home, no evil could touch her.

I don't say such things as I stroke her fingers.
Instead I say, as her eyes widen with wonder:
"Every night during your ten years in this world
As you sleep I enter the bull ring with my sword
To stand where your mother would have stood:
A gladiator standing guard, a secret matador."

Girl, Fifteen, Walking in Ronanstown

I am walking and I shall keep walking,
Past the gangs clustered on the corners
With nothing except catcalls and jeers,

Past shuttered shops where we kissed,
Past graffiti-strewn lanes we haunted
Before his betrayal soured their magic.

I am walking past interrogating stares,
An inquisition of girls with know-all eyes.

I am Nicky-No-Name, declining all labels,
Walking tall because I know my own worth.

I refuse to look down and refuse to look back,
I shiver from the cold but feel no regret,

Because I carry my destination in my heart,
Even if I lack the words to express it yet.

Graffiti on a Corner

Each time I pause at this corner
It unlocks a private code:
Myriad labyrinths of memories
Flash past along the road.

The thrill of being chased, first kiss,
First time to encounter love:
You may see a bare street corner,
I glimpse a treasure trove.

Passing Certain Estates

On the night that they announce his death
Those of us who live in the homes he built
Will throng the gates that guard his mansion.

We will carry his oak coffin on our shoulders
In a silent procession through every estate
Where he ignored bylaws, left roads incomplete.

We shall dig a grave to half its legal depth
And lower his casket as far as it will fit,
Promising to return and complete the task.

His coffin shall be left jutting out on a slope,
And on his subsiding headstone will be writ:
*"Death too has short cuts and sharp practices,
I lie as I left you, betrayed by empty promises."*

Great War Triptych

(Knocklyon House, Dublin, 1917 & 2007)

1

Telegram boys were harbingers,
    Carriers of despair,
Bearing news of local boys barely
    Older than they were,
Down lanes in Ballyboden, Ballyroan,
    Whitechurch and Old Bawn:
Mothers in windows, transfixed to stone,
    Begging them to cycle on
Past their homes with the envelope
    Whose formulaic words
Extinguished the compulsive hope
    That was like an addiction,
As they beseeched God that the telegram
    Was about someone else's son.

11

These are the gates where the telegram boy stopped,
The window beneath which he crossed the gravel.
No sniper's bullet could be as loud as his knock.

Grief drifted in, shapeless as mustard gas, to linger
Along every muted corridor in Knocklyon House,
Sleet drummed against the slates like skeletal fingers.

The Great War spread from France and the Dardanalles
To requisition cottages in Tallaght and Rathfarnham,
Conscripting mothers once addicted to novenas

But now trapped in a No Man's Land of mourning.
A clock ticking off the infinity of empty afternoons,
A war against despair to be fought every morning

When it felt so easy to simply cave in and surrender.
The battlefront changes, yet a great war continues in rooms
Once filled with longing for a son missing in Flanders.

People wonder how they survived, having lost friends,
How they will endure another sleepless night of combat
Against desires that scratch and claw at nerve ends,

Against dark angels incessantly whispering in their minds,
That one drink, one hit, one bet, one click will do no harm,
How they will endure the void of leaving their fix behind.

111
Addicted people learn to cope, pacing corridors
    Where a dead boy's parents grieved:
Wounds raw, nerve ends jangling, desperate for
    Something that cannot be retrieved.
People who endured delirium tremors, endured detox,
    Suffered such symptoms of withdrawal
That they think they only imagine the elderly couple
    Quietly observing them in the hall,
Ghosts who survived, who came through anguish,
    Even if the yearning never retreated.

Knocklyon House in Knocklyon, Dublin, was the family home of a First World War soldier who died in the Ypres Salient in 1917 and whose body was never recovered. Today the house is used as the Rutland Centre for Addiction.

The Cut

When the cut is decided four decades from now,
Should I prove to be the final golfer standing

I will leave for my friend a wooden tee neatly broken:
His Indian sign left behind to mark each perfect drive.

I will leave for my brother a ball miraculously perched
On the edge of an unplayable hazard, just within bounds,

Sitting up with such incongruous temptation in the rough
That some stranger cannot resist playing it when found.

For my brother-in-law I will leave a discarded cigarette butt
Nonchalantly smouldering on the fringe of a deserted green,

After being tossed away to allow him slay another par putt.

(Fourball, Edmondstown Golf Club, Rathfarmham
Founded by the Jewish Maccabean Society, 1944.)

Figure Walking in Autumn Storm, Marley Park

Without your love I am a suspended soul in limbo,
The beat of a butterfly with one wounded wing,

The eye that has lost any horizon on which to fix,
The lexicon stripped of every definition of purpose,

The voyage with no charted course, the sleeping pill,
The satellite no longer moored by gravitational pull,

The speck of rock trundling through empty galaxies,
The singular coffee cup, the timber futon's assembly,

The bedroom door upon which I am afraid to knock,
The chestnut found by no hand amid autumn grass

Pining for the soft skin that enveloped him in the husk,
That moistly expanded to encompass his growing flesh,

The other that he never knew he was separate from,
Until it fell and split wide open on the concrete.

Put your lips against mine and I will come to life
Put your lips to mine and I will be made complete.

Put your lips to mine and I will be held secure
No matter what illness comes or what calamity,

If I were wrapped up inside your love once more
Then no evil on this earth could ever harm me.

Conquistador, Pilgrim Soul

Three times I have sacrificed myself as a martyr,
Given up my life so that others might escape,

Three times this week I was betrayed by daybreak,
Three times I rose again to reboot my computer.

This is my life, or dare I say, my true existence.
Their world of enduring eight hours in an office

Before queuing twice a week in this evening traffic
To study in the Tallaght IT, no longer feels realistic.

Reality only starts when I arrive home to my duplex,
To dine with a plate placed in front of the screen,

When I anticipate the unknowns that may occur,
When I decide what universe I intend to inhabit,

When I prepare to play games against strangers
And to off-load real estate in my cyber abode.

In the IT they think me peculiar, call me a loner,
But I am far from alone. A world-wide web of us

Refuse to recognise their restrictions and borders
On who we are and who we are allowed become.

I know where I belong and it is not amid this traffic.
Like my grandmother, I believe in another existence,

But while she filled her heaven with plastercast saints
I populate mine with sinners, fantasists and dissidents.

My parents believe in nothing but the news on television.
"You're twenty-four", they say, "you know nothing yet."

But I know that their universe is the ultimate illusion,
With everything rationalised and carefully packaged

And all eventualities covered by an insurance plan.
Anyone can find me in my world and yet no one can,

There are no lanes cordoned off by traffic cones
But infinite space to be whoever I decide that I am.

I have personalised my private version of heaven:
It resonates with mythic beings, living and dead.

I know my visitors only as whom they claim to be.
Perhaps the driver opposite me in this tailback

Visited my site last night pretending to be a girl?
Maybe that is his reality, made flesh in one click?

Perhaps only the lies we concoct are actually true,
Because we select them by our own free choice:

Our true skin colour, true sex and true voice.
I was given no say in my nationality or birth,

But in cyberspace I make these choices myself,
Floating free of restrictions imposed on earth.

At the screen I can become my own creator,
I can discover the true core of my soul,

There I can become all the parts of myself,
Indivisible at last, finally made whole.

Wedded

(For Bernie)

This is what I am wedded to:
The bus journey in the dusk,
Tailbacks, roadworks, queues,
Tired faces staring into space
Thrown forward in our seats
As the driver applies the brakes,
Glimpses into strangers' lives
As they chat on mobile phones.

The name carved on a boulder
At the entrance to our estate,
The sweep of curving rooftops,
The bicycles left on the path,
Hopscotch marked out in chalk.

The light in the kitchen window
When she gets home before me,
The bustle of pots, the radio
Blathering about the outside world,
A scent of spices as she says hello,
Busy stirring a dish at the stove.

The voice of the woman I wed,
Who makes every aspect blessed,
This kitchen, this suburban street,
This bus trip like a pilgrimage
Back to where I may finally lie
With my bride amid shoals of roofs,
Amid the vast galaxies of estates,
Amid the myriad specks of light,
In the place where I am safe,
Where I wake deep in the night
And touch her sleeping face.

Silent couple in a red car, leaving Old Bawn

I no longer know how to try and recapture
The intimacy which once existed between us,

So harmoniously woven that we barely noticed
The coded rituals of touch holding us together.

One night we forgot to close the fridge door
And by morning a small transparent glacier

Had enveloped our kitchen, edging upstairs
So that we woke inside an ice-capped world.

We remain the same people, except that now
We can watch every breath we take harden

Like a slow spectre formed by ectoplasm
In this arctic atmosphere. I feel scared

Because once you said that you could not live
Here on this earth without me by your side,

But each breath shows you no longer depend
On my love to exist. If I died you would survive,

Because you are ready to step from our capsule
Amid the rooftop galaxies, too absorbed to notice

My hands banging against the small glass porthole
As you cut the cord, drifting free into the universe.

The Absent Fathers

I am the smiling man letting go his hand at the door,
Timing to the last second when I must bring him back.

I am the six days of purgatory when I torture myself
With longing for a glimpse of his eight-year-old face.

I am a succession of happy meals and playgrounds,
An opened wallet, a question he cannot express,

An extra portion of fries, a man trying not to obsess
About making each moment we spend together count.

I am the cause of confusion, I am a boundless love,
I am a blemish in what should be his fairytale world.

I am the father who only catches glimpses into his life,
I am a monthly standing order, a hunter with his gun

Who lost his way out hunting, a sailor adrift at sea
Outside a Clondalkin house, meekly awaiting my turn.

I am a weekly routine, a slot allotted by a mediator,
A concerned voice unable to discern if he is all right,

I am the name that he has learnt not to call out for:
The absence who cannot banish his fears at night.

Things He Will Miss...

His son growing in time to look like him;
The way that his girlfriend's face will age;

How they will finish building Clondalkin;
How other racers' memories of him will fade

Until his name becomes a mere postscript,
With younger drivers oblivious to his feats

As they video each other turning doughnuts,
Cocooned behind tinted glass and sun strips.

How the buzz fades from woofers and wheelspins
When one night you cease to feel indestructible;

How sons are meant to shoulder their parents' coffins
Not leave them to shoulder the ache of absence.

He will miss his son playing football in the park,
Cadging cash for dates, slagging his music tastes.

He will miss hearing the boy drive off into the dark,
The purgatory of night hours spent lying awake.

Flowers Mark the Spot

Flowers mark the spot
Of the stolen car's somersault.
Flowers mark the spot
Of another unprovoked assault.
Supermarket bouquets,
Barely noticed, wrapped in plastic,
Held aloft by sellotape
Where a girl sought her fix,
Where lovers found a body
Whose hands were neatly tied,
Where a driver lost control,
Where someone's daughter died.

Bouquets that disintegrate
During months devoid of sleep,
When numb parents ache
To hear again a key turn in a lock
As loved ones arrive home
Having dodged the roulette of fate.

Withered flowers represent
A grief they can never articulate.

Haulier passing The Red Cow Roundabout, 11.15pm

I just want to be home, is that too much to ask?

Even when asleep I see white lines, hard shoulders,
Automated cranes on foreign wharves loading ships,

I see that final container that I still have to deliver,
The one that always seems to keep me from home,

I see tailbacks and blockades and upturned wreckage,
Docksides where I smoke when sleep refuses to come.

The blonde teenage hiker incessantly pulling a comb
Through her hair as she climbed up into my truck,

Strung out on heroin, falling asleep on my shoulder
With the same smile as my thirteen-year-old daughter.

Man Walking on Monastery Road, Clondalkin, 2.15 a.m.

You knew once what it felt like to truly be loved,
To belong absolutely with another presence:
A sense so intense you grew barely aware of it.

But now you sense it acutely by its absence,
By her indifference when you lie segregated
In the cold war zones of a partitioned mattress.

You know it's gone because you're stricken with panic,
Invisible, bereft of worth, feeling that you do no exist
Because you no longer see yourself reflected in her iris

Enlarged by love, held secure there, made complete.
You are two commuters now who fleetingly meet
On route to the bathroom or breakfast counter.

And tonight it feels like thirty years has dissolved,
Once again you're a youth adrift on neon-lit streets,
The young man who thought he was rescuing her,

The young man whom she rescued from loneliness,
The lost soul, exploring lanes, reluctant to turn home,
Resurrected inside the old man you've suddenly become.

Jesus of Clondalkin

Maybe Jesus is wandering these roads tonight,
Unrecognised, unacknowledged, utterly alone,

Passing half built apartment blocks investors own,
Passing burnt-out cars, glass shards, twisted chrome,

Threading a path through Neilstown and Quarryvale,
In Dunnes Stores white socks, with his jacket torn.

Maybe we are so adrift in our own cares that we fail
To see whip marks, collapsed veins, his crown of thorns.

Possibility

Just leave yourself open to the possibility
That one dawn you wake to find your mind clear,

One dawn you win back the love you derailed,
One dawn you will kick the habit of blaming yourself.

One dawn you will wake to hear a clear signal,
A wavelength unmuffled by interference or static,

You will recognise the DJ's voice as your own
Advertising a unique extravaganza treasure hunt
Where each clue is a signpost through your past.

You will walk through a maze of sleeping estates,
Collecting golden tickets concealed amid mistakes
You made when addiction stopped you thinking straight.

That dawn, when figures emerge amidst the chaos,
You will walk forward, unafraid to embrace happiness.

III

The Frost is All Over

For Tony McMahon and David Power

Tuning Up

In kitchens and pub corners and concert halls
Musicians gather. They open instrument cases,
Tune up, exchange greetings, gossip and jibes
Until, gradually, the noise of everyday life ceases.

At some unspoken moment they become someone other
Than who they were when walking through the doors.
Nobody mentions it, but the mood subtly alters
Just like the mood switches between two lovers

When one takes the lead, drawing the curtains tight
To initiate the change. A taut electricity in the air
Dissipating sharp words, healing perceived slights,
Suspending all cares in the expectant atmosphere.

The musicians arch their fingers, purse their lips,
Pause for one last second, then, tantalising slow,
Fingers and lips allow the tune to find its shape
And steadily grow towards its lingering crescendo.

"Culna Dear, Don't Come Any Nearer Me..."

You can never claim to own this tune,
But, with luck, it may come to own you
For brief seconds in the midst of playing
When everything else is stripped away
Except the bare skeleton of the notes,
That gradually you find a way to clothe
With emotions only music can express.

Your fingers no longer feel like your own,
You have become a servant, a medium,
Allowing a procession of ghosts to slip
Through the buttons of your accordion:
The hag with the golden sovereigns
Standing amid a white sea of bog cotton,
And the singer with a craggy Connemara face,
Closing his eyes in an American city to summon
The young lover tapping at the windowpane,
The girl chiding him, yet wanting him nearer,
Both caught up in the breathless love chase.

Seamus Ennis in Drumcondra

I see him leave that flat we shared
And walk down Home Farm Road,
Black coat buttoned against the wind,
A countryman's hat pulled down,
And in his hand a battered case,
Containing the set of uilleann pipes
Found in fragments by his father
In a sack in a London pawnbrokers:
A jigsaw nobody could piece together
A hundred years after they were crafted
By Coyne of Thomas Street in Dublin.

He carries his case like a secret dossier
That no passer-by could decode
As he boards a bus into the city
Unnoticed among the evening hordes.
Times are hard, our flat threadbare,
He survives on tins of steak and kidney pie,
On meals that he cooks at odd hours,
When he tells yarns and truly comes alive.
There is rent to pay, a meter to be fed,
Afternoon visits to the local launderette
Nights of wind rattling the rotting windows,
When he spreads his coat over his bed.

This is the price of making music,
Of living the life for which he was born,
He is on his way that night to perform
For little pay to a meagre audience
In the back room of a Dublin pub,
With a television blaring in the lounge.

Ignoring the jarring cash register,
Three dozen people sit, transfixed,
By a set of reels learned from his father
Interlaced with grace notes and tricks
Picked up from pipers who are ghosts,
Who died recorded only by himself,
Who never learnt music, wrote nothing down,
But carried the tunes in their minds,
Knowing that with their own deaths
Dozens of nameless reels would also die.
Ennis plays with due respect for the dead,
In his one good suit, a white shirt and tie.

Recording

This is the sole recording they persuaded her to make.
Listen closely and you will hear beneath the static
The clock in her hillside kitchen, the spitting fire
Set because so many neighbours were bound to arrive,
A door opening unexpectedly, a tramp of hobnailed boots
Ushering a man in from the yard, his low voice apologetic.

And behind him, beyond the thick-set windows panes,
Winter wind and rain amid the bent shoulders of trees
And, even more faintly, the hum of an engine running
To charge the batteries powering the revolving spools
Of the reel-to-reel tape machine in her gas-lit cottage,
Where she has made tea for strangers and neighbours,

Apologised for the pot-holed lane and shocking weather,
Discussed local deaths, the electric wires creeping closer,
When finally, reluctantly, with almost shy reverence,
She has taken her grandfather's fiddle from the wall,
And started to play the tunes he taught her as a girl.

Bold Doherty

Mary Ann Carolan sings in old age on the Hill of Rath,
She sings of Bold Doherty, that hard-drinking man,
She sings for her mother who taught her this song,
She sings for the collector who tracked her down,
A young man with a bouzouki from her native town,
She sings to fill out the years this song was unheard,
She sings to reflect the depth of life she has known,
She sings for a young girl who has not yet been born,
A child who late one night will hear an old woman
Sing on the radio and fall in love with the words:
A punk-haired girl who will later travel the world,
To conjure up Bold Doherty's drunken wanderlust
In a blue spotlight, white hands clasping the microphone,
A stranger in a strange time making this song her own.

O'Neill's Cavalcade

It takes the bones of a lifetime to learn to play,
To probe your way into the soul of the tune,
To show the notes enough respect to open up
So that a line of ninety-nine ghosts march forth:

The retreating chieftain and his cavalcade,
The moonlit ships, their white sails raised:
With unbowed swagger, vowing to return,
Defiant exiles gaze back at a shrinking land.

Sport

The sport of dancer's boots striking the floor,
The sport of hands clasped, a gasp for breath,
The flying trail of sparks from nails on stone,
The secretive slipping past crowds at the door;
The cold night air, the waving trees overhead
In sheltering ditches, in deserted city lanes,
The chase, the catch, the lingering first kiss
Under a crescent moon, the stars gargantuan,
Her dark hall door, blood pulsing with music,
Her eyes gone serious, her bedroom light dim.

Sonny Brogan's Jigs

At eighteen you discovered how Leitrim was located,
Anonymously and miraculously, amid a labyrinth

Of small North Dublin streets of red-brick terraces,
Down which musicians slipped with instrument cases.

The old countryman welcoming you at his hall door,
A magnolia painted parlour, ablaze with evening light,

Where every Sunday flotillas of musicians gathered
For sessions that gathered pace until late at night.

Box players from Limerick, a fiddler from Kilrush,
Student teachers whose concertinas had been seized,

Pipers who wanted bodhráns played only with billhooks,
And sean-nos singers home from labouring jobs in Leeds.

The way Sonny Brogan could conjure a sense of Leitrim,
By playing unadorned sets of jigs on his accordion,

As sparse and crisp as a hillside white with frost,
As exhilarating as walking a girl home in the dark.

Candles of horse chestnut above the college walls,
Emigrants on open-backed buses bound for the boat,

College life, mysteries of bra straps and Cavan girls,
Sweat on dance club walls, Brilcream, saxophones,

And a passport every Sunday into a different world
When musicians gathered in Sonny Brogan's home.

The Piper Patsy Touhey plays in Cohen's Variety Show, New York, 1905

Somewhere between the vaudeville skits and slapstick fare,
Amid the heat and grease-paint of Cohen's Irish emporium,

When coarse laughter stops and cat calls quieten down,
I stare towards the dark pit that contains my countrymen,

And, striping away jaunty tricks and frilly showmanship,
I play in the style of my father who died when I was ten,

Coughing blood in a tenement amid the maelstrom of Boston,
In a flat smaller than the cabin we left behind in Loughrea.

I've told stage-Irish jokes until punters can laugh no more,
I have used darting triplets to backstitch notes that soar

High in staccato pitch before lunging down towards hell,
Like those sea voyage in steerage amidst endless swells,

With no land yet in sight and a famished land left behind.
But now amid the growing silence as I stare into the pit,

I play this slow air for my father and for my father's kind,
Who close their eyes and recognise their own grief in it.

The Frost is All Over

(i.m. Seamus Ennis, piper & collector)

At Christmas in the cottage bearing his name
A packed crowd sways as musicians play.
The Naul village is quiet, a sky bereft of stars
Breathes webs of frost on windscreens of cars.
Awakened by the tunes he once collected
The bronze statue of the piper under the tree
Stirs himself, his stiff fingers elongated
As he lifts the chanter and pipes off his knee
And takes a cautious step across the square.
In his coat pocket a half-bottle of whiskey,
In his head the notes of thousands of airs
Still jostle and cling to life in his memory.

Songs collected in Irish clubs and building sites,
In Birmingham and Brixton, Battersea and Crewe,
White shirted men softly playing the squeeze box,
Lonely men singing about the Sweet Mountain Dew
Between shifts at the Vauxhall car plant in Luton;
Men, who once laboured with asphalt and asbestos,
Rasping out final breaths in flats in Camden Town
With the district nurse their sole weekly caller;
Men who tuned to Radio Eireann in kitchenettes
Hemmed in by foreign voices through cavity walls,
Desperate to hear a fiddle amid the static and forget
The damp odour of exile and the cross of loneliness.

The ghosts swarm to join him in the frosted square
Like they swarmed as boys to hiring fairs in Strabane
And queued on Dublin quays to board cattle boats
And waited at dawn in Kilburn for contractors in vans.
A lifetime of being herded and praying to be chosen,
Of pints and tin whistles shyly produced at gatherings.

Remember me, one of them begs the bronze figure,
You recorded me one December in Wolverhampton,
You came back to my bedsit, the only soul I ever let in.
I sang with my eyes closed amid my few possessions,
And it felt like I had only to reach out through the dark
And every face I left behind would be there to touch.

Play The Bucks of Oranmore, play The Frost is All Over,
Play for ghosts eternally condemned to be The Wild Rover.
Play for those picking mushrooms in the fields of Athenry
From Estonia and Lithuania, from Lagos and Paraguay.

Remember us, Seamus, we entrusted you with song
In Yorkshire mill towns that never felt like home.
Our legions left no footprints amid the wet cement
But you drank with us and gave our songs worth
In bothies on farms in Strathclyde and Arbroath.
We wander in limbo now, the forgotten remnants
Of an army recruited from hillside and tenement
To go abroad and send home a weekly remittance.
Strap on your pipes, Seamus, as each ghost flits
Around your cottage window to hear our tunes
Renewed in the young musicians' fingers and lips.

"O'Neill's Music of Ireland"

When you play this air I live again in every breath,
In how you bend a note, in how our fingers overlap
A century apart, bound together by incomprehensible
Sets of squiggles a Chicago Police Chief jotted down
After I helped unload a cargo steamer on the wharf.

The longshoremen tipped me a wink to take a break
Because they were in awe of Chief O'Neill's uniform
And relieved that he had not come to arrest anyone.
How cold the tin whistle felt as I took it from my shirt,
Blowing away ice with a blast that seemed to summon

Fellow Irish dock workers who clustered, bewildered
That such a big brass would waste his time to record
Some inconsequential tune I first heard as a child,
So long ago I'd almost lost the memory of being scared
At a wake until a woman soothed me, humming its air.

Some immigrants argued about the tune's real name,
Others grew angry, urging me to play a music hall song,
As if I was dragging us back to the poverty we fled from.
They stood, cowed and sullen, as if accused of a crime
Best forgotten, with my notes taken down in evidence.

The notes I played that afternoon on the freezing wharf,
The notes a woman crooned to a scared boy at a wake,
The notes a cop pressed between the pages of his book,
The notes you now play, the notes you unconsciously hum
When you pace the floor at night, soothing your infant son.

The Nomad

Always in my mind the landscape of Waterford
Awaits beyond the boundaries of foreign towns.
On childhood nights I swore one day to explore
High into the wilds of the Knockmealdowns,
To see Dungarvan, Passage East and Tramore:
Places sounding distant and impossibly strange.

No encounter has quenched the sense of wonder
That fuelled this life of hostels and train stations,
A life spent seeking a home, yet needing to wander,
Never able to settle on one job, one lover, one abode,
Imagining that beyond the next set of mountains,
The next city block, I'll discover a narrow road

Beckoning in the dark between hawthorn bushes,
To a bend where I will stare up at an attic window,
To see a child's face looking out into the darkness,
Listening to his mother sing in the kitchen below,
His hands at the glass pane, his gaze rapturous,
Already in his mind a nomad, a wandering hobo.

IV

Three Poems

First Book
(For June, Deirdre & Roger)

Soon my mother will return with the promise of a comic
For her child confined to bed with a lit fire in the grate.

Lace curtains cast studs of light on rose-patterned wallpaper
As girls are summoned into a skipping rope's arc at our gate.

Although told to remain in bed, curiosity tempts me to explore.
On top of the wardrobe I find the only two books in the house.

One is made of gold-sprayed metal, with a slot for coins and a lock:
Housewife's Savings Book. Property of the Munster & Leinster Bank.

I shake the half-crowns inside, then take down a tattered hardback.
Feeling grown up, I open this present from an aunt to my sister.

Some pages are torn, childish squiggles disfigure the inside cover.
I struggle with turns of phrase, the otherness of each character:

Nurseries and governesses, proving yourself *"a chum worth having".*
In retrospect, this may be the worst children's book ever printed,

But I find myself outside the lit window of a house in Suffolk,
The curtain is drawn back to let me peer, with shy bewilderment,

Into another universe, incomprehensibly alien, but I am hooked:
I might be the stammering child, the soft prey, the class dunce;

But I have stumbled into a sphere where bullies cannot threaten,
Turing each mildewed page, I start to inhabit two worlds at once.

In Memory of George Best

In one corner of our mind it remains 1969:
Frosted pavements, icy breath, yet our hands thaw

In the thrill of chasing a ball under streetlights,
Voices in the dark calling the names of Best and Law.

A drudge of decades have clogged our arteries,
Yet no matter what occurred, what we have become,

When we see again his feint, his sheer artistry
Thousands of us are instantaneously made young.

Carmen's Garden in Flanders

Not only ghosts of soldiers cross the battlefields
Which factories and streets now cover over:
Other lives led here were no less extraordinary,
The life of every wife, every lost child or father.

Among the poppies their Forget-Me-Nots grow.
Grief will never halt; her loss will remain forever.
Forget-Her-Enough to relinquish mourning though:
An evening must come when you enter the garden

Planted by a lost one amid what was once trenches.
Lift your face into the rain and grasp these seconds
Because rain will never come like this again, seeping
Into roots of plants, into crevices thronged by finches,

Onto insect-lined stems, as life ceaselessly reawakens,
Even amidst the unassailable void death leaves behind.